KILLER ANIMALS

KILLER WHALES

ON THE HUNT

REVISED EDITION

by Janet Riehecky

Reading Consultant:
Barbara J. Fox
Reading Specialist
North Carolina State University

Content Consultant:
Deborah Nuzzolo
Education Manager
SeaWorld, San Diego

CAPSTONE PRESS
a capstone imprint

Blazers is published by Capstone Press,
1710 Roe Crest Drive, North Mankato, Minnesota, 56003
www.mycapstone.com

Library of Congress Cataloging-in-Publication Data is available on the Library of Congress website.
ISBN: 978-1-5157-6240-9 (revised paperback)
ISBN: 978-1-5157-6241-6 (ebook pdf)

Editorial Credits
Abby Czeskleba, editor; Bobbi J. Wyss, book designer; Kyle Grenz, set designer;
Svetlana Zhurkin, media researcher

Image Credits
Dreamstime: Serena Livingston, 8-9; Getty Images: Paul Nicklen, 10; iStockphoto:
Cullenphotos, 27, Douglas Wilson, 16-17, Grafissimo, 13; National Geographic Creative:
Brian J. Skerry, 14; Seapics: Amos Nachoum, 24-25, Doug Perrine, 22-23, Jasmine
Rossi, 18-19, 21; Shutterstock: David Pruter, Cover, Doptis, 28-29, Tatiana Ivkovich, 4-5,
vladsilver, 6-7

Printed and bound in the USA.
009969R

TABLE OF CONTENTS

SEAL HUNTING

A **pod** of killer whales slowly swims through the water. The whales see a seal sitting on a sheet of ice.

pod — a group of whales

The killer whales surround the sheet of ice. They **spyhop** in the water and make waves. The waves wash the seal off the ice. One of the killer whales tears the seal apart.

spyhop — a whale behavior in which the whale pokes its head out of the water

Killer whales attack all animals, including great white sharks.

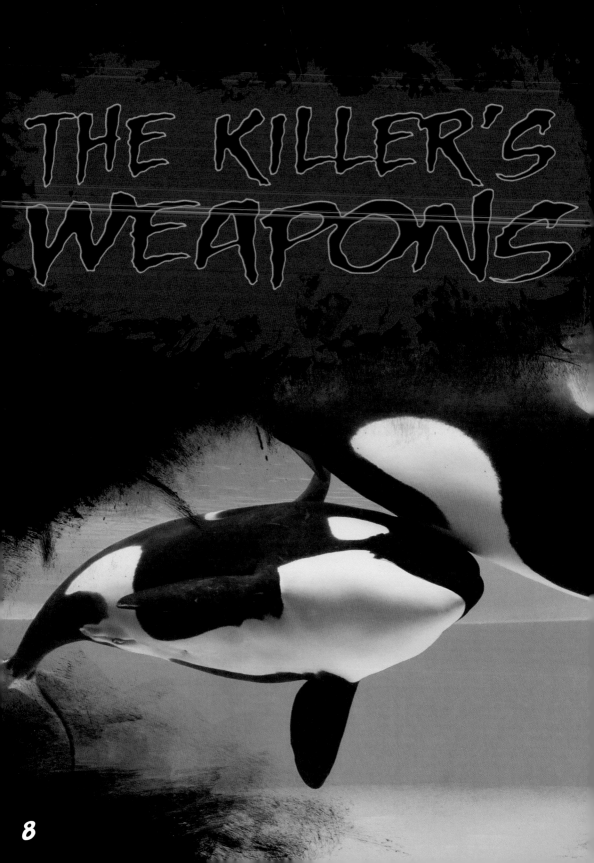

THE KILLER'S WEAPONS

Killer whales are the largest members of the dolphin family. Females grow to be more than 15 feet (4.6 meters) long. They weigh about 8,000 pounds (3,629 kilograms). Males are longer and heavier than females.

Killer whales make loud clicking noises to find **prey**. Sounds bounce off objects in the water. Whales use sounds to figure out an animal's size. Killer whales can also tell if an animal is far away.

prey — an animal hunted by another animal for food

Killer whales have more than 40 sharp, pointed teeth. Their teeth rip meat from the bodies of animals. Each tooth is about 3 inches (7.6 centimeters) long.

KILLER FACT

Killer whales do not use their teeth to chew meat.

The tail of a killer whale is large and strong. Killer whales have two **flukes** on their tails. Killer whales slap prey with their tails. Slapping can hurt or kill animals.

KILLER FACT

A killer whale's flukes have no bones.

fluke — the wide, flat area at the end of a whale's tail

A FIERCE HUNTER

Killer whales search the ocean for prey. The whales can swim as fast as 30 miles (48 kilometers) per hour.

KILLER FACT

Killer whales may eat more than 300 pounds (136 kilograms) of meat a day.

Killer whales often hunt together. Sometimes a pod of killer whales surrounds prey. Killer whales may also trap an animal against a cliff. The whales easily move in for the kill.

Killer whales slide on land to grab an animal. They pull animals into the water. Sometimes they toss their prey into the air.

KILLER FACT

Mothers show their young how to hunt by pushing them onto the beach.

Killer Whale Diagram

tail fluke

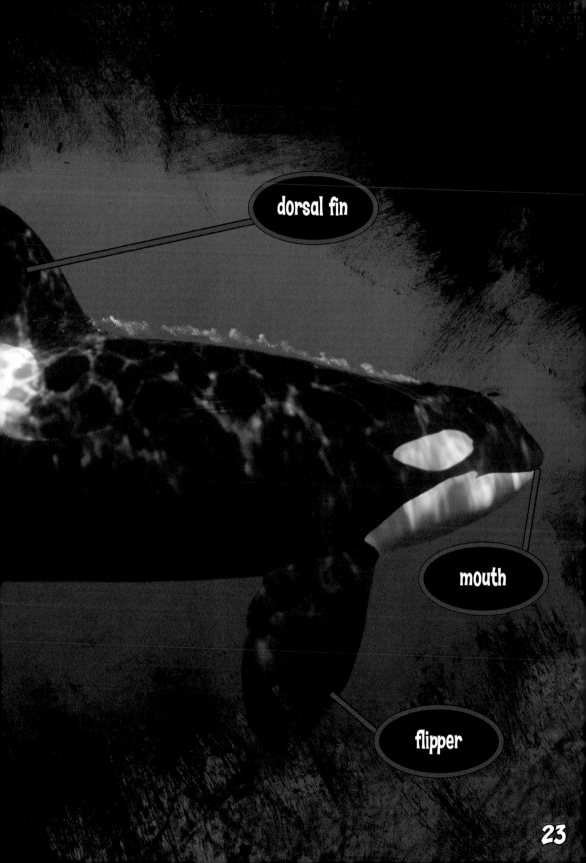

dorsal fin

mouth

flipper

23

HELPING THE ECOSYSTEM

Killer whales balance the **ecosystem** by eating fish, seals, and sea lions. Killer whales help lower the number of animals. Too many animals of one kind can hurt the ecosystem.

ecosystem — a group of animals and plants that work together with their surroundings

People don't usually hunt killer whales. But people can still hurt them. Trash dumped in the ocean can be dangerous to killer whales. The oceans need to stay clean so that killer whales can stay healthy.

KILLER FACT

A killer whale's top fin is called the dorsal fin. Male killer whales can have dorsal fins up to 6 feet (1.8 meters) tall.

Out of the Water!

GLOSSARY

ecosystem (EE-koh-sis-tuhm) — a group of animals and plants that work together with their surroundings

fluke (FLOOK) — the wide, flat area at the end of a whale's tail; whales move their flukes to swim.

pod (POD) — a group of whales; pods range from less than five whales to more than 30 whales.

prey (PRAY) — an animal hunted by another animal for food

spyhop (SPYE-hop) — a whale behavior in which the whale pokes its head out of the water

READ MORE

Adelman, Beth. *Killer Whales.* Boys Rock! Chanhassen, Minn.: Child's World, 2007.

Malam, John. *Killer Whales.* Scary Creatures. Danbury, Conn.: Franklin Watts, 2008.

Rake, Jody Sullivan. *Killer Whales Up Close.* Whales and Dolphins Up Close. Mankato, Minn.: Capstone Press, 2009.

INTERNET SITES

FactHound offers a safe, fun way to find Internet sites related to this book. All of the sites on FactHound have been researched by our staff.

Here's all you do:

Visit *www.facthound.com*

FactHound will fetch the best sites for you!

INDEX